D1095768

A CHILD'S PRAYERS

A
CHILD'S
PRAYERS

*Beautiful Prayers for
Every Occasion*

With Color Illustrations
by VIVIAN SMITH

Selected by Bette Bishop

HALLMARK EDITIONS

ACKNOWLEDGMENTS

"Just for Jesus" from Poems for Peter, by Lysbeth Boyd Borie. Copyright 1928, 1956 by Lysbeth Boyd Borie. Published by J. B. Lippincott Company.

"How Nice" from A Child on His Knees by Mary Dixon Thayer. Reprinted with permission of The Macmillan Company. Copyright 1926 by The Macmillan Company. Renewed 1954 by the author.

"Prayer on Christmas Eve" by Nancy Byrd Turner, reprinted with permission of the author.

"A Great Gray Elephant" reprinted with permission of the National Society for the Prevention of Blindness, Inc.

A CHILD'S PRAYERS

——————— ❋ ———————

Father, We Thank Thee

Father, we thank Thee for the night
And for the pleasant morning light;
For rest and food and loving care,
And all that makes the world so fair.

Help us to do the things we should;
To be to others kind and good;
In all we do, in work or play,
To grow more loving every day.

     Amen.   Kate Douglas Wiggin

A Child's Morning Prayer

I thank Thee, Lord, for quiet rest,
    And for Thy care of me:
Oh! let me through this day be blest,
    And kept from harm by Thee.

Oh, let me love Thee! kind Thou art
    To children such as I;
Give me a gentle, holy heart,
    Be Thou my Friend on high.

Help me to please my parents dear,
    And do whate'er they tell;
Bless all my friends, both far and near,
    And keep them safe and well.
        Amen.   Mary Lundie Duncan

Children's Prayer

Make me, dear Lord, polite and kind
  To every one, I pray.
And may I ask You how You find
Yourself, dear Lord, today?
    Amen.   John Bannister Tabb

Thank You, God

Thank You for the world so sweet,
Thank You for the food we eat,
Thank You for the birds that sing,
Thank You, God, for everything.
    Amen.

A Prayer of Thanks

Thank You for the bread we eat,
Our homes and families,
    the friends we meet,
And thank You for each glad new day
And for Your kind and loving way.
    Amen.

Grace Before Meals

Thank You, Lord,
For food so good
And help me eat it
As I should.
    Amen.

Grace

Be present at our table, Lord;
Be here and everywhere adored.
Thy creatures bless, and grant that we
May feast in Paradise with Thee.
    Amen.   John Wesley

A Child's Grace

God is great and God is good,
And we thank Him for our food;
By His hand we must be fed,
Give us, Lord, our daily bread.
    Amen.

Thank You, Lord

What God gives, and what we take,
'Tis a gift for Christ, His sake:
Be the meal of beans and peas,
God be thanked for those, and these:
Have we flesh, or have we fish,
All are fragments from His dish.

      Amen.   Robert Herrick

Prayer After Meals

The blessing of God rest upon all those
who have been kind to us, have cared for us,
have worked for us, have served us, and
have shared our bread with us at this table.
Our merciful God, reward all of them in Your
own way ... for Yours is the glory and the
honor forever.

      Amen.   Saint Cyril of Alexandria

Grace Before and After Meat

Bless me, O Lord, and let my food
strengthen me to serve Thee,
for Jesus Christ's sake.

Amen.   The New England Primer

Praised Be Thou, O Lord

Praised be Thou, O Lord our God,
    King of the universe,
Who causest the earth to yield
    food for all.
    Amen.   Hebrew Blessing

13

Grace for Children

I fold my hands and bow my head,
And thank You for my daily bread.
    Amen.

Lord, We Thank You

Lord, we thank Thee for this place in which
we dwell; for the love that unites us; for
the peace accorded us this day; for the
hope with which we expect the morrow; for
the health, the work, the food, and the
bright skies that make our lives delightful;
for our friends in all parts of the earth,
and our friendly helpers.
    Amen.   Robert Louis Stevenson

Bless Us, O Lord

Bless us, O Lord, and these Thy gifts
which we are about to receive from Thy
bounty, through Jesus Christ, Our Lord.
Amen.

We Give Thee Thanks

We give Thee thanks for all Thy benefits,
Almighty God, through Christ, Our Lord.
Amen.

Teach Me to Pray

Lord, teach a little child to pray,
And then accept my prayer,
Thou hearest all the words I say
For Thou art everywhere.

A little sparrow cannot fall
Unnoticed, Lord, by Thee;
And though I am so young and small
Thou dost take care of me.

Teach me to do the thing that's right,
And when I sin, forgive;
And make it still my chief delight
To serve Thee while I live.

      Amen.   Jane Taylor

Stay By My Side

Stay by my side, dear God above,
Protect and guide me with Your love,
Forgive me for bad things I do
And help me to be more like You;
Protect my parents, stay by their side,
Be near my friends to guard and guide,
Bring love to children everywhere
And keep them in Your tender care,
And with each morning, let the sun
Bring warmth and joy to everyone.

Amen.

God Bless Everyone

God bless the skies above
And everything below,
God bless everyone I love,
And everyone I know.

Amen.

For Children in Other Lands

For children who live in other lands,
I offer up a prayer
That God will bless them every day,
And keep them in His care.
      Amen.

A Great Gray Elephant

A great gray elephant,
A little yellow bee,
A tiny purple violet,
A tall green tree,
A red and white sailboat
On a blue sea —
All these things
You gave to me,
When You made
My eyes to see —
Thank You, God!
    Amen.

A Little Child

Lord, help me by Thy grace to be,
Lowly and kind of heart like Thee;
Gentle and loving, meek and mild,
Thy servant, though a little child.
        Amen.   *Isaac Watts*

20

For Guidance

Dear God, be good to me—
the sea is so wide and my boat
is so small.

      Amen.   Prayer of the Breton Fishermen

Hear Thy Children

O God our Father, Thou hast promised
to hear Thy children when they pray
to Thee. Teach us how to pray, and
what to ask for. Help us to mean
what we say ; and give us grace to
love Thee more, and to love the
people for whom we pray, for Jesus
Christ's sake.

      Amen.

A Prayer for Asking

Please give me what I ask, dear Lord,
If You'd be glad about it,
But if You think it's not for me,
Please help me do without it.
                Amen.

Jesus, Tender Shepherd

Jesus, tender Shepherd, hear me;
Bless Thy little lamb tonight;
Through the darkness be Thou near me,
Keep me safe till morning light.

All this day Thy hand has led me,
And I thank Thee for Thy care;
Thou has warmed me, clothed and fed me;
Listen to my evening prayer!
                Amen.   Mary Duncan

Care for Me

God who holds the children dear,
Care for me and keep me near.
What my worth and what my fortune,
All rests gently in God's hands.
Fortune comes and fortune goes,
But he who loves God fortune has.

Amen.

Swedish Prayer

The Lord's Prayer

Our Father which art in heaven,
   Hallowed be thy name.
Thy kingdom come,
   Thy will be done in earth,
as it is in heaven.
Give us this day our daily bread.
And forgive us our trespasses,
As we forgive those who trespass
   against us.
And lead us not into temptation,
but deliver us from evil:
For thine is the kingdom,
   and the power, and the glory,
for ever.
     Amen.   St. Matthew 6:9-13

Thank You for My Parents

Thank You for my parents, Lord,
Who love and care for me,
Take them in Thy loving arms
And keep them close to Thee,
Help me, Lord, to find new ways
To show my love for them,
New ways to make them proud of me
And happy, too.
    Amen.

My Friend Next Door

Thank You for my friend next door
And my friend across the street,
And please help me to be a friend
To everyone I meet.
     Amen.

A Prayer for Those Dear to Me

God bless all those that I love;
God bless all those that love me;
God bless all those that love those
    that I love,
And all those that love those
    that love me.
     Amen.

From an old New England sampler

To Follow Thee

O Holy Jesus,
Most merciful Redeemer,
Friend and brother,
May I know Thee more clearly,
Love Thee more dearly,
And follow Thee more nearly.
      Amen.   st. Richard of Chichester

Prayer for People Everywhere

O Blessed Lord, please hear my prayer
  And help all people be
Kind and good to everyone,
  And live in peace with Thee.
      Amen.

Thou Hearest

Father, I thank Thee that Thou hast heard me.
I knew that Thou hearest me always.

    Amen.   John 11: 41-42

Thank You, God, for My Family

Thank You, God, so very much
   For my family;
Bless them, please, and make them all
   As happy as can be.
    Amen.

For Everything

For making me healthy, making me strong,
So I can run and play all day long,
For giving me eyes so I can see
All the good things You have made for me,
For a mouth to speak and two hands to touch,
For everything, Jesus, thank You so much.

     Amen.

What Can I Do for You, God?

What can I do for You, God,
I, who am still so young?
I can love those around me;
One can love, though small.

I shall try to please
By doing kindly things.
I shall help my mother;
One can help, though small.

I shall love my friends,
My sister and my brother.
I shall play with all in friendly ways;
One can be kind, though small.

And when they smile at me
I know that You are near.
Help me to show Your love
Each day to those I meet.
I send my prayer to You;
One can pray, though small.
   Amen.

━━━━ ✿ ━━━━

Lullaby

Fourteen angels round my bed,
Watch beside me through the night;
Two at my feet, two at my head,
Two at my left, two at my right,
Two to cover me, two to wake me,
Two to Paradise to take me.

From the Flemish

Just for Jesus

Jesus, I kneel down to say
Thank You for another day,

For hands to feel and eyes to see
And all Your loving gifts to me.

Teach me in Your words to talk
Help me in Your ways to walk,

Guide and bless me from above,
Jesus, it is You I love!

Amen.   Lysbeth Boyd Borie

Child's Evening Hymn

Now the day is over,
Night is drawing nigh,
Shadows of the evening
Steal across the sky.

Jesus give the weary
Calm and sweet repose,
With Thy tenderest blessing
May our eyelids close.

Through the long night-watches
May Thy angels spread
Their white wings above me,
Watching round my bed.

When the morning wakens,
Then may I arise
Pure and fresh and sinless
In Thy holy eyes.
                Amen.   Sabine Baring-Gould

34

Evening Prayer

Thank You, Jesus, for today,
For friends and family, work and play,
Keep me, Jesus, through the night,
Wake me with the morning light,
And when tomorrow comes, I pray,
Help me please Thee all the day.

   Amen.

An Evening Hymn for a Little Family

Now condescend, Almighty King,
    To bless this little throng;
And kindly listen while we sing
    Our pleasant evening song.

Before Thy sacred footstool, see
    We bend in humble prayer,
A happy little family,
    To ask Thy tender care.

May we in safety sleep tonight,
    From every danger free,
Because the darkness and the light,
Are both alike to Thee.
        Amen.   Anne and Jane Taylor

Prayer for Friends

Thank You for friends who share my fun.
Please watch over them, each one.
Help me, Lord, to gladly share
And teach me always to be fair.
      Amen.

Now I Lay Me Down to Sleep

Now I lay me down to sleep,
I pray Thee, Lord, my soul to keep;
Thy love stay with me through the night
And wake me with the morning light.
I ask not for myself alone,
But for Thy children, every one.
      Amen.

Prayer for a Child

When it gets dark the birds and flowers
Shut up their eyes and say goodnight,
And God who loves them counts the hours,
And keeps them safe till it gets light.

Dear Father, count the hours tonight
While I'm asleep and cannot see:
And in the morning may the light
Shine for the birds, the flowers, and me.

    Amen.   William Hawley Smith

I Thank Thee

I thank Thee for the love so true
That watched o'er me the long day through.
Dear Saviour, keep me through the night
And wake me with the morning's light.
　　　Amen.

Child's Good Night Prayer

Father, unto Thee I pray,
Thou hast guarded me all day;
Safe I am while in Thy sight,
Safely let me sleep tonight.
Bless my friends, the whole world bless,
Help me to learn helpfulness;
Keep me ever in Thy sight:
So to all I say goodnight.
　　　Amen.

How Nice!

How nice it is, dear God, to know
That You make all the flowers grow!
How nice it is to stop and think
You made the spring from which I drink!
How nice it is to know that You
Painted the sky that lovely blue!
How nice it is to know You fill
The night with stars and always will!
But O! How nice to know You made
Me, too! Sometimes I am afraid
I do not thank You as I should—
You are so wise, dear God, and good!

      Amen.   Mary Dixon Thayer

God's Gift

For life and health and strength
    I thank the Father kind;
I cannot count His mercies o'er,
    So many gifts I find.

The wee bird has its nest,
    Safe in the trees so tall,
For birdlings' nests, for children's homes,
    I thank the Lord for all.
        Amen.

God Giveth All Things

We thank our loving Father God,
Who gives us everything,
Who sends the sunshine and the showers,
And makes rich harvest spring.
He clothes the lilies of the field,
He feeds each bird and beast;
And all may share His tender care,
The greatest and the least.
        Amen.

Prayer for Springtime

For all the pretty flowers that bloom,
For all the birds that sing,
For grass that grows so soft and green,
For all the joys of spring,
    We thank Thee.
        Amen.

Prayer for Summer

For summer's days so full of fun,
For fleecy clouds and pleasant sun,
For lakes and rivers, grass and trees,
Thank You, Lord, for all of these.
    Amen.

Thank You

Thank You for giving me eyes to see
The wonderful world You made for me,
Thank You for giving me legs to run
Through the wind and rain and sun,
Thank You for giving me fingers to touch
Soft kittens and puppies I like so much,
Thank You for giving me those I love
And for watching over me from above.
    Amen.

We Thank You, Lord

Lord Jesus,
We have so much to thank You for—
The sun that fills the world with light,
The stars that twinkle in the night,
The flowers that bloom, the grass that grows,
Shady trees, the wind that blows,
Fields and streams, all this and more—
We have so much to thank You for!
        Amen.

Prayer for Autumn

Thank You, God, for autumn,
With its clear and frosty air,
And with its pretty leaves
That scatter color everywhere.
        Amen.

Prayer for Winter

I thank Thee, Lord, for winter,
With its snow and frosty air—
For those who love and keep me—
For this nice, warm house we share;
I give Thee thanks, O Father,
And pray to Heaven above
To guard me through the winter
With the warmth of Thy dear love.
     Amen.

The Moon

I see the moon,
And the moon sees me;
God bless the moon,
And God bless me.
      Amen.   Celtic child's saying

Good Night Prayer

Good night! Good night!
Far flies the light;
But still God's love
Shall flame above,
Making all bright.
Good night! Good night!
      Amen.   Victor Hugo

————— ☼ —————

My Birthday Prayer

I pray that on my birthday
The Lord above will bless
Me and all my family, too,
With every happiness.
    Amen.

Thank You for My Birthday

Thank You for my birthday
And for my presents, too,
And thank You, God, for making me
So happy all day through.
Now that I am older,
There's so much I want to do
To help my friends and family
And by doing so, please You.
    Amen.

Prayer for Easter

I hear the bells of Easter ring:
Thou art risen, Lord and King!
Thou art risen to the skies:
To Thy throne, my prayers arise.
Amen.

Prayer for a Friend at Easter

Jesus, our dear Master, came
To preach the gospel in God's name.
He blessed the little children too,
And led His flock as shepherds do!

Always meek, yet always strong,
Loving truth, rebuking wrong,
By His own life, He showed the way
That we should live from day to day!

And now that Easter Day is near,
That lovely, happy time of year,
May Christ, Our Saviour, be with you
And keep you safe the whole year through!
Amen.

An Easter Prayer

May Christ, Who rose on Easter Day,
Bless all I love, for whom I pray.
Amen.

As Thyself

Lord Christ, Thou gavest Thyself for me;
Behold here I am,
And here I give myself to Thee.

      Amen.   Jeremiah Dyke

For All Thy Love

We thank Thee, then, O Father,
   For all things bright and good,
The seed time and the harvest,
   Our life, our health, our food;
Accept the gifts we offer,
   For all Thy love imparts,
And, what Thou most desirest,
   Our humble, thankful hearts.

      Amen.   Matthias Claudius

Prayer on Thanksgiving Day

Just as the Pilgrims thanked You, Lord,
For all You gave to them,
So today we bow our heads
And thank You too.
       Amen.

To Serve Thee

O holy Jesus, who led the Wise Men by a
star, draw me unto Thee that I may worship,
love and serve Thee for evermore.

Amen.

Loving Jesus

Loving Jesus, meek and mild,
Look upon a little child!

Make me gentle as Thou art,
Come and live within my heart.

Take my childish hand in Thine,
Guide these little feet of mine.

So shall all my happy days
Sing their pleasant song of praise;

And the world shall always see
Christ, the Holy Child, in me.

Amen.   charles wesley

Away in a Manger

Away in a manger, no crib for a bed,
The little Lord Jesus
    laid down His sweet head.
The stars in the sky
    looked down where He lay,
The little Lord Jesus, asleep on the hay.

Be near me, Lord Jesus, I ask Thee to stay
Close by me forever, and love me, I pray;
Bless all the dear children
    in Thy loving care,
And take us to heaven,
    to live with Thee there.
            Amen.   Martin Luther

A Welcome Song

Oh, Lord Jesus, on this day
    That You were born so far away
I raise my voice and gladly sing
    A welcome song to You, our King!
    Amen.

What Can I Give Him?

What can I give Him
Poor as I am?
If I were a shepherd,
I would give Him a lamb,
If I were a Wise Man,
I would do my part,
But what can I give Him?
Give my heart.

Christina G. Rossetti

Prayer on Christmas Eve

O wondrous night of star and song,
  O blessed Christmas night!
Lord, make me feel my whole life long
  Its loveliness and light!
So all the years my heart shall thrill
  Remembering angels on a hill,
And one lone star shall bless me still
  On every Christmas night!
      Amen.   Nancy Byrd Turner

O Holy Jesus

O holy Jesus, once a little Child for us,
help us to remember the Manger at Bethlehem,
and always to bring to Thee lowly, loving
and grateful hearts.

     Amen.

New Year Prayer

I fold my hands in humble prayer
To ask You for Your loving care—
Please keep me safe, be ever near
Throughout the bright and glad new year.
Amen.

To Care for Me

The old year left us
   in the night,
The new year came
   with morning light;
Whatever it holds,
   Lord, may You be
Nearby to watch
   And care for me.
Amen.

Holy Child

O Holy Child of Bethlehem,
Descend to us, we pray;
Cast out our sin, and enter in,
Be born in us today.
Amen.

Phillips Brooks

Set in 12 point Joanna, a light roman of
remarkable clarity, especially suitable
for children's reading, created in 1930
by Eric Gill. The display lines are set in
the Bauer Elizabeth italic. Typography
by Saul Marks set at the Plantin Press.
Designed by Harald Peter.